EARLY AMERICAN STENCIL DESIGNS

Charlene Tarbox

DOVER PUBLICATIONS, INC.
NEW YORK

Note

In an all-new collection, New York City artist, fabric designer, teacher and author Charlene Tarbox presents in stencil images some of the most popular designs of the early nineteenth century.

Based on stencil patterns found on the walls and floors of early American homes, quilting and textile designs, wood carvings, hand-decorated trays and furniture, these designs are reminders of the detail and charm that characterized much nineteenth-century craftsmanship. Seventy-eight pages of patterns—flowers, birds, farm animals and geometric shapes—make *Early American Stencil Designs* an invaluable resource for decorators, artists and hobbyists alike.

Copyright

Copyright © 1994 by Dover Publications, Inc.
All rights reserved under Pan American and International Copyright Conventions.

Published in Canada by General Publishing Company, Ltd., 30 Lesmill Road, Don Mills, Toronto, Ontario.
Published in the United Kingdom by Constable and Company, Ltd., 3 The Lanchesters, 162–164 Fulham Palace Road, London W6 9ER.

Bibliographical Note

Early American Stencil Designs is a new work, first published by Dover Publications, Inc., in 1994.

DOVER *Pictorial Archive* SERIES

This book belongs to the Dover Pictorial Archive Series. You may use the designs and illustrations for graphics and crafts applications, free and without special permission, provided that you include no more than ten in the same publication or project. (For permission for additional use, please write to Dover Publications, Inc., 31 East 2nd Street, Mineola, N.Y. 11501.)

However, republication or reproduction of any illustration by any other graphic service, whether it be in a book or in any other design resource, is strictly prohibited.

Library of Congress Cataloging-in-Publication Data

Tarbox, Charlene.
　　Early American stencil designs / Charlene Tarbox.
　　　　p.　　cm. — (Dover pictorial archive series)
　　　ISBN 0-486-27968-5 (pbk.)
　　　1. Stencil work—United States. 2. Decoration and ornament, Early American. I. Title. II. Series.
　　TT270.T37 1994
　　745.7'3—dc20
　　　　　　　　　　　　　　　　　　　　　　　　　　93-34609
　　　　　　　　　　　　　　　　　　　　　　　　　　CIP

Manufactured in the United States of America
Dover Publications, Inc., 31 East 2nd Street, Mineola, N.Y. 11501

3

11

29

41

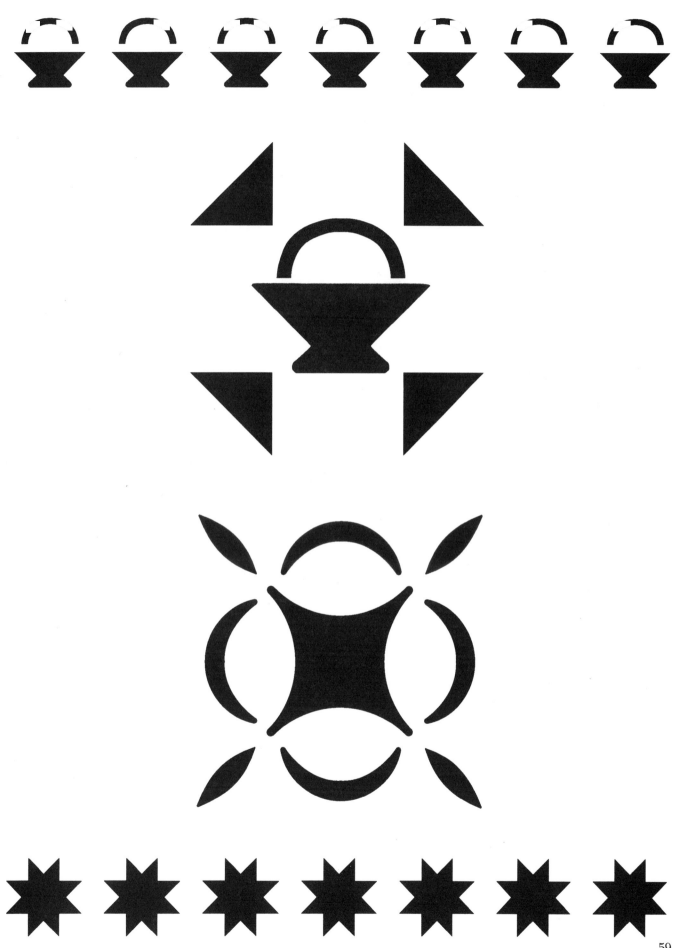

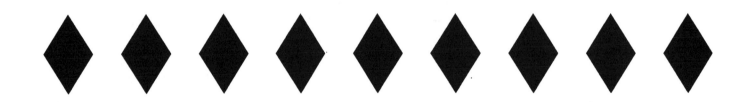

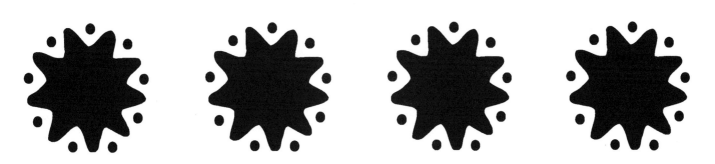